Dr. Wernher von Braun: A Short Biography

Pioneer of Rocketry and Space Exploration

By Doug West, Ph.D.

Dr. Wernher von Braun: A Short Biography
Pioneer of Rocketry and Space Exploration

Table of Contents

Preface

Welcome to the book, *Dr. Wernher von Braun: A Short Biography*. This book is part of the 30 Minute Book Series and, as the name of the series implies, if you are an average reader this book will take around 30 minutes to read. Since this short book is not meant to be an all-encompassing biography of Wernher von Braun, you may want to know more about this man and his accomplishments. To help you with this, there are several good references at the end of this book. Thank you for purchasing this book and I hope you enjoy your time reading about this legendary innovator.

Doug West
August 2017

Introduction

Wernher von Braun, born in East Prussia to the European aristocracy just before the onslaught of World War I, became a rocket and space travel enthusiast while still a young lad. His early experiments promoted him to the position of the German Army's top civilian rocket specialist at only 20 years old. He continued his work under the Nazis through World War II, establishing a secret rocket base at Peenemünde on the German coast of the Baltic Sea. He led the group that developed the V-2 rocket that terrorized London during the closing year of the war. As the war drew to a close and Germany gave up the fight, von Braun and his rocket team surrendered to the Americans, rather than to the Russians. After the war, von Braun and his group put their expertise to work for the U.S. Army at Fort Bliss in the arid south Texas desert. At first the Americans weren't sure what to do with their newly acquired team of German rocket scientists, engineers, and technicians. As the Cold War between the Soviets and America heated up, von Braun and his team would be key to helping America keep up with the rapidly evolving threats presented by the Russians.

America responded to the launch of the *Sputnik* satellite by the Russians in 1957 with a massive buildup in the areas of science and technology. The race to space had begun in earnest and von Braun would be in the middle of it, leading the Marshall Space Flight Center in Huntsville, Alabama, to develop the rockets that would thrust America into outer space. As director, he would guide the design and development of the giant Saturn rockets that would carry the Apollo module with three astronauts to the Moon. Continue reading this short biography and learn the story of the dreamer of space that helped put a man on the Moon.

Chapter 1 - Early Life

"For my confirmation, I didn't get a watch and my first pair of long pants, like most Lutheran boys. I got a telescope. My mother thought it would make the best gift." - Wernher von Braun

Wernher Magnus Maximiliam Freiherr von Braun was born on March 23, 1912, in a noble family from Wirsitz, Posen Province, in the former German Empire. Von Braun's father, Magnus Freiherr von Braun, was an influential conservative politician, serving as a Minister of Agriculture during the Weimar Republic, while von Braun's mother, Emmy von Quistorp, was the descendant of a medieval European royal family. Philip III of France, Robert III of Scotland, and Edward III of England were her ancestors. Wernher was the middle child with two other brothers — one of whom would follow him into rocketry.

As a child, von Braun developed a passionate interest in astronomy after his mother bought him a telescope for his confirmation gift. In 1915, the family moved to Berlin as Magnus was appointed Minister of the Interior. Wernher's adeptness in engineering and his interest in rockets became evident at the age of 12 when he and his older brother built a rocket powered wagon with large fireworks. The two wheeled the wagon onto an upscale Berlin street, lit the fuses, and watched the action. Von Braun recalled the incident years later:

"I was ecstatic. The wagon was wholly out of control and trailing a comet's tail of fire, but my rockets were performing beyond my wildest dreams. Finally they burned themselves out with a magnificent thunderclap and the vehicle rolled to a halt. The police took me into custody very quickly. Fortunately, no one had been injured, so I was released in charge of the Minister of Agriculture — who was my father."

Besides his interest in science, von Braun was also a great pianist with the ability to play Bach or Beethoven from memory. After learning to play several instruments from an early age, he was so immersed in music that he expressed his desire to become a composer.

In 1925, von Braun enrolled at a boarding school at Ettersburg Castle near Weimar. Despite the family's expectations, he had mediocre results as a student, particularly in physics and mathematics. During his time there, he met the pioneer rocket scientist Hermann Oberth, who had published one of the first works on rockets entitled *By Rocket Into Planetary Space*. In 1928, von Braun changed schools, moving to the North Sea island of Spiekeroog. His interest in rocket engineering became his main focus and he decided to advance his knowledge of physics and mathematics.

In 1930, von Braun enrolled at Technische Hochschule Berlin, where he became a member of the Spaceflight Society. The university offered him tremendous opportunities when it came to his childhood dream of working on rocketry and spaceflight, as he assisted in the testing of the liquid-fueled rocket motor under the supervision of scientist Willy Ley.

Von Braun graduated in 1932 with a degree in mechanical engineering, convinced, however, that the applications of engineering technology were not enough to make space exploration a reality. He decided to continue his studies at the University of Berlin, where he took advanced courses in physics, chemistry, and astronomy. In 1934, a thesis entitled *Theoretical and Experimental Contributions to the Problem of the Liquid-Propellant Rocket* gained him a Ph.D. in physics from the University of Berlin. His concentration had been aerospace engineering and his innovative thesis was classified by the German military and not published until 1960. Although most of his work focused on military rockets, von Braun remained primarily interested in space travel throughout his studies. He was a keen admirer of Hermann Oberth and Auguste Piccard, the pioneer of high-altitude balloon flight.

In 1933, while von Braun was still working on his doctorate, the National Socialist Germany Party came to power in Germany, and rocketry became a significant point of interest in the national agenda, being sponsored through generous research grants. Von Braun began to work at a solid-fuel rocket test site in Kummersdorf. At the end of 1937, von Braun and his fellow research partners successfully launched two liquid fuel rockets that reached heights of over one mile.

Von Braun's rocketry team continued their research, investigating different types of liquid-fueled rockets in aircraft. Von Braun started to work with pilot Ernest Heinkel, telling him during a flight test that he would not only become a famous man but that von Braun would help him fly to the Moon. In June 1937, a flight test at Neuhardenberg proved that an aircraft can fly propelled by rocket power alone. Von Braun's engines were powered by liquid oxygen and alcohol and used direct combustion. Around the same time, Hellmuth Walter began experimenting with hydrogen peroxide based rockets that were superior and more reliable than those of von Braun's.

As a rocketry researcher and engineer, von Braun was an admirer of the American Dr. Robert H. Goddard and his innovative work in rocket science. German engineers occasionally contacted Goddard to ask for advice regarding technical issues. Goddard was very secretive with his work on rocketry and provided little assistance to the Germans. Nearly all of Goddard's rocket patents were not available to the Germans during World War II as the U.S. government classified them to limit their distribution, thus hindering the German rocket development program.

Chapter 2 - World War II

"Crash programs fail because they are based on the theory that, with nine women pregnant, you can get a baby a month." - Wernher von Braun

As the interest in rocketry continued to escalate within the German military, a permanent home was found for von Braun and the rocketry team. In 1937, Peenemünde, on the island of Usedom along the Baltic Sea coast was selected. This location would become the secret site for Hitler's regime to undertake development of military rockets. Von Braun and most of the Kummersdorf scientists and engineers made the transition to Peenemünde. It would take two years of construction before the base would become fully operational. When completed, it became a secret center, complete with housing, offices, laboratories, factories, and before the war would end, a forced-labor camp with barracks for several thousand prisoners.

As the build up at Peenemünde continued, Adolf Hitler was beginning to aggressively acquire real estate at the cost of Germany's neighboring countries. By 1939, the Germans had acquired control of the Rhineland, Austria, and Czechoslovakia. In September of 1939, Germany invaded Poland without a declaration of war. The German air fleets destroyed Poland's scant air force on the ground before it could rise to flight to defend the country. Just two days after Germany's invasion of Poland, France and Great Britain declared war on Germany. What would turn out to be history's deadliest conflict between nations had begun.

As the technical director at the Army Rocket Center at Peenemünde, von Braun's work was of great interest to the high-level officials of the Nazi regime. His refusal to join the Party would have been the end of his career and von Braun was unwilling to give up his work. In an article from 1952, von Braun admitted that by playing by the rules, his life under the totalitarianism rule of the Nazis had been rather good.

Figure – Von Braun (in suit) with Nazi officers in 1941

Together with a large team of engineers and scientists, von Braun began to work on developing liquid-fuel rocket engines specifically designed for aircraft. In 1942, von Braun showed Adolf Hitler a movie with the takeoff of an A-4 (which was later renamed the V-2) rocket and Hitler, delighted by the work of the young engineer, promoted him to professor, an exceptional honor as von Braun was only 31 years old. Despite the success of the rocket, von Braun was disillusioned that his work was used for warfare instead of space travel. He was heard saying that he would have preferred to see his rockets land on another planet, not kill people.

As the demand for more V-2 rockets increased at Peenemünde, the program developed a shortage of workers. To solve the labor shortage, SS General Hans Kammler, the engineer behind many of the concentration camps built by the Nazis, suggested using camp prisoners as slave laborers in the program. The chief engineer of the V-2 rocket factory, Arthur Rudolph, agreed to the proposal. Many people died in conditions of torture, extreme brutality, and exhaustion during the construction of the V-2 rockets. There is now evidence that 20,000 people died because of the intolerable working conditions at the camp. Although von Braun visited the Mittelwerk site several times and agreed that the work conditions at the plant were harsh, he never seemed to have understood the magnitude of the atrocities. In 1944, he realized that deaths had indeed occurred on multiple occasions. A Buchenwald inmate later claimed that von Bran went to the concentration camp to choose slave laborers and that he passed by the corpses of people tortured to death on his frequent visits to the camp, yet he never seemed to notice. In his writings, von Braun confessed that he was aware of the work conditions, but felt unable to change anything. Friends of von Braun admitted hearing him talk about Mittelwerk and describing the place as "hellish." He had also told his friends that when he tried to talk to an SS guard about his treatment of the laborers, the guard threatened him. Von Braun's team member, Konrad Dannenberg, was convinced that if von Braun had protested against the brutality of the SS, he would have been shot.

Von Braun had been under surveillance since October 1943, after he and two of his colleagues were heard expressing regret about not working on a spaceship and talking about the possibility of losing the war. The discussions between von Braun and his colleagues suggested a defeatist attitude, which was not regarded well by the regime. The SS grew increasingly suspicious of von Braun. Since von Braun had access to airplanes, the Gestapo worried that he could easily escape the country. In a report issued about him, von Braun was also falsely accused by Himmler himself of being a communist sympathizer who tried to sabotage the rocket program. Von Braun's relationship with the Nazi regime thus took an unexpected turn. On March 14, 1944, von Braun was taken into custody by the Gestapo and imprisoned at Stettin (now Szczecin, Poland) where he was held for two weeks without knowing the charges against him. Senior Nazi party members convinced Hitler to release von Braun so he could continue to lead development of the V-2 program without delay.

The V-2 rocket stood 46 feet tall and was fueled by ethyl alcohol and liquid oxygen. The rocket was guided in flight by a three-axis gyro-pilot actuating steerable exhaust vanes and aerodynamic surfaces on the fins. A successful missile could travel nearly 200 miles reaching a height of 50 miles halfway to the target. The rocket engine burned out when the speed was approximately 3,500 mph; the unlucky souls at the receiving end heard both a sonic boom and an explosion. Even without an explosive warhead, a V-2 crashing to Earth would leave a crater 45 feet deep and 120 feet across!

The V-2 rocket did not have a significant impact on the outcome of World War II. Though the rocket was a major advancement in technology and could be quite deadly when it hit the target, not enough rockets were produced and launched to change the tide of the war.

Figure - A German V-2 rocket fired by the British
from a launch pad near Cuxhaven in Germany
during Operation Backfire in 1945

In November 1937, von Braun became an official
member of the National Socialist Party, although his
relationship with the Nazi regime was very complex
and ambivalent throughout the time. He did not
engage in political activity, but in a 1952 article,
von Braun confessed that he had strong patriotic
feelings and was influenced by the promises of the
Nazis to restore Germany's greatness. The post-
World War I reparations imposed by the Treaty of
Versailles had resulted in ruinous inflation and
economic depression for the country.

After the Second World War, when von Braun was living and working in the United States, he wrote about his impressions of Hitler during the war:

"I met Hitler four times. When we met in 1934, he seemed a pretty dowdy type. Later, I began to see the shape of the man — his brilliance, the tremendous force of personality. It gripped you somehow... My first impression was that here was another Napoleon, another colossal figure who had upset the world... At my last meetings with him, Hitler suddenly struck me as an unreligious man, a man who did not feel that he was answerable to anyone, that here was no God for him... He was wholly without scruples, a godless man who thought himself the only god, the only authority he needed."

In 1940, von Braun joined the Allgemeine SS, the major paramilitary organization of the Nazi Party, where he was given the rank of Untersturmfuhrer (Second Lieutenant). He later explained that SS leader Himmler sent him a firm invitation to join the SS, promising him that he did not have to fulfill any tasks that would take him away from his rocketry work. Von Braun complied with the request and was promoted three times and in June 1943, he became a SS-Sturmbannfuhrer (Major). Numerous photographs from that period show von Braun in the company of SS members, wearing the SS uniform. However, he repeatedly claimed that he did not have any direct involvement in politics. Moreover, his promotions had been simply technical, as he received the news each year by mail.

Chapter 3 - Surrender to the Americans

"We can lick gravity, but sometimes the paperwork is overwhelming." - Wernher von Braun

By early 1945 it was obvious that Germany was losing the war as the Allied forces advanced upon the nation. Von Braun and his planning staff were in Peenemünde, less than one hundred miles away from the Soviet Army. While the Soviet Army was getting closer, von Braun and his staff realized that their only option was to surrender, preferably deciding in advance how and to whom to surrender to make sure they would receive protection. Since surrender to the Soviets was not a pleasant perspective for von Braun, he and his staff decided that surrendering to the Americans would be the best thing to do.

Von Braun and his advisers hatched a plan to retreat to the Harz Mountains, which would put them closer to the Americans. On official SS stationary, von Braun wrote himself bogus orders to move some five thousand personnel, scientific equipment, documents, and V-2 parts by truck, train, and automobile. The convoy traveled to their new temporary home by night to avoid Allied aircraft attack. During a night drive at high speed, his driver fell asleep at the wheel and the resulting accident killed the driver and severely broke von Braun's left arm. As he was unwilling to spend time in the hospital to properly heal, the neglected broken arm caused complications and had to be re-broken to realign his bones a month later.

Figure - General Dornberger (left) and Wernher von Braun, arm in cast from an auto accident, after surrendering to American forces in 1945

The missile team's first stop was at the underground Mittelwerk missile factory. The group settled into abandoned factories and other empty buildings. The armada of a thousand trucks and dozens of trains had transported thousands of personnel, tons of missile assemblies, machinery, and documents to this interim location.

In mid-March new orders came down from SS General Hanskammler, who was in charge of Peenemünde and the V-2 production facility at Mittelwerk. Army Major General Dornberger, von Braun, and five to six hundred of the best technical people were to move further south to Oberammergau, situated in the northern foothills of the Bavarian Alps. They were also ordered to destroy V-2 blueprints, production drawings, and other secret documents. Instead, Dornberger and von Braun had the precious paperwork hidden in abandoned mines in the area.

At Oberammergau, the group was housed with SS security guards in barracks surrounded by barbed-wire fences. Rumors circulated through the camp that the SS high command was prepared to liquidate the rocket team rather than have them captured by the enemy. Von Braun was able to reason with the SS that it would be advantageous for the group to disperse out into the surrounding villages rather than being bunched together and making an easy target for an Allied bombing raid.

The SS security guards saw the logic in von Braun's argument and Dornberger, von Braun, his brother Magnus, and two dozen colleagues, along with their guards, relocated in early April to a resort hotel. Von Braun later recalled of this time:

"There I was, living in a ski hotel on a mountain plateau. There were the French [forces] below us to the west, and the American to the south. But no one, of course, suspected we were there. So nothing happened. The momentous events were being broadcast over the radio: Hitler was dead, the war was over, an armistice was signed — and the hotel service was excellent."

With news of the death of Hitler, the SS guards disappeared, attempting to blend in with the civilians, leaving the rocket team to fend for themselves. On May 2, 1945, the day following the public announcement of Hitler's death, Magnus von Braun headed down the mountain road looking for Americans. Two miles into his trek he encountered an advance antitank patrol unit and told the solders in broken English: "We are a group of rocket specialists up in the mountains. We want to see your commander and surrender to the Americans." The officer in charge was apparently unaware of the quest for the V-2 team and told Magnus to come back tomorrow with the leaders of the team. At first light the next day, the von Braun brothers and other key team members drove down the mountain to surrender to the Americans. Soon more than four hundred of von Braun's teammates were taken into custody, questioned, and moved to Bavaria.

Chapter 4 - Career in the United States

"It will free man from the remaining chains, the chains of gravity which still tie him to this planet." - Wernher von Braun

The U.S. Army was instantly aware of what a valuable, yet unexpected catch von Braun and his fellow engineers were. The Army had already had von Braun at the top of the Black List, a list of German top scientists and engineers whom the U.S. military experts wanted to interrogate. As the leader of the team, von Braun was interrogated by British and American intelligence officials. The first to interview von Braun were British scientists, including Britain's leading rocket engineer, L.S. Snell, who would later invent the engines for the supersonic Concorde jet liner. The British officials were eager to talk to von Braun as they were aware that the U.S. would later deny them access to him. The transcripts of the interviews remained top secret, inaccessible to the other allies.

The U.S. Secretary of State approved the relocation of von Braun and his team to the United States, yet the news reached the public months later, after the U.S. intelligence agencies created false biographies for them, removing affiliations to the Nazi Party from their records. The U.S. government proceeded to grant them permission to work in the country. Part of the Peenemünde staff was settled in

Aberdeen Proving Ground in Maryland, while von Braun and the remaining members of the team were transferred to Fort Bliss, near El Paso, where the Army had a large installation.

The German engineers found the living conditions at Fort Bliss to be rough and von Braun later admitted that he found it difficult to develop any sort of emotional attachment to his new home. The hot desert-like conditions of Fort Bliss, in deep southern Texas, were very different from the intercostal island the rocket team had grown accustomed to. After having thousands of engineers working for him at Peenemünde, von Braun was now working with the American Jim Hammil, a 26-year-old major with an undergraduate degree in engineering, who refused to call him professor and never complied with von Braun's requests for new materials. Because of their political status, von Braun and his colleagues could only leave Fort Bliss with a military escort.

The Germans were under one-year contracts working as Department of the Army Special Employees — and were, according to the government "wards of the Army." The group had not passed through immigration and possessed neither passports or visas. They worked first as rocket consultants to the U.S. military and then as technicians and teachers in assembly and launch of captured V-2 rockets. For more than a year, their presence was kept secret from the American public.

At Ford Bliss, von Braun and his team took the mission of training military and industrial personnel in the field of rocketry and military applications, such as guided missiles. They became involved in the Hermes project, where they had the task of helping an American team to refurbish and prepare V-2 rockets shipped from Germany for re-launching. However, their main interest was to study the potential of rockets in the development of military and research applications.

Chapter 5 - Promoter of Space Exploration

"There is just one thing I can promise you about the outer-space program — your tax-dollar will go further." - Wernher von Braun

The first few years at Fort Bliss were a period of professional stagnation for von Braun and his team. Without a serious missile development or space program, the United States was not sure what to do with their team of German rocket scientists. Things started to change in 1949 when a series of international events put America on notice as the Cold War between the Soviet Union and the United States was starting to take shape. The Soviet Union was starting to test atomic weapons, and intelligence reports revealed that the Soviets had developed powerful rockets that were capable of carrying large payloads over great distances. During this period things were starting to heat up on the Korean peninsula. The communist controlled North Korea was becoming aggressive to the Western leaning South Korea.

The heightened world tensions prompted the United States to begin serious development of their own large rockets capable of carrying heavy payloads. The military sought a home for the new rocket program and decided on a mothballed World War II base in northern Alabama for the new program. Shortly after plans were finalized to relocate the

German scientists, engineers, and technicians to Huntsville, Alabama, von Braun made a visit to the area and reported back to his colleagues: "Oh, it looks like home! So green, green, everything is so green, with mountains all around!"

For von Braun and the rocket team, the move to Huntsville, Alabama, was much less of an adjustment than the move to El Paso from Germany. Once in place at the Redstone Arsenal located in Huntsville, von Braun kept pursuing his goal to use rockets for space exploration. Although busy with leading military rocket development, von Braun continued to hope that he could one day use the rockets for achieving humankind's dream of conquering space.

When his work became better known in the United States, von Braun realized that his position allowed him to popularize his ideas. The headline of the *Huntsville Times* from May 14, 1950, "Dr. von Braun Says Rocket Flights Possible to Moon," was the daring beginning of a new adventure. Two years later, von Braun made public his concept of a manned space station in a series of articles, "Man Will Conquer Space Soon," published in *Collier's Weekly*. Illustrated by artist Chesley Bonestell, the articles were instrumental in putting von Braun's ideas into public circulation. Von Braun sought the help of fellow scientist Willy Ley, whom he had met at the University of Berlin. In the United States, Ley was an accomplished science writer and space advocate and he helped von Braun publish his concepts. Highly technical, von Braun's concepts were an example of fine innovative engineering and even anticipated technical aspects of space flight that became real many years later. Von Braun wanted his space station to work, most importantly, as an assembly platform for manned lunar missions. He was aware that his space station could be armed with missiles and adapted for warfare, yet he expressed in his writings that he considered military applications dreadful and worrying.

Von Braun had covered every detail of a possible lunar expedition, not leaving anything to chance. He saw these expeditions as massive undertakings, with 50 astronauts traveling in two spacecraft and a third spacecraft carrying the cargo, each spacecraft propelled by a rectangular array of 30 engines. According to von Braun's strategy, astronauts had to establish a permanent base in the Sinus Roris area of the Moon and explore the surroundings in pressurized rovers for at least eight weeks, making sure to reach the crater Harpalus and the Mare Imbrium hills.

Figure - This is a von Braun space station concept. In a 1952 series of articles written in *Collier's*, Dr. Wernher von Braun wrote of a large wheel-like space station in a 1,075-mile orbit.

Von Braun's visions did not stop here as he also worked on developing concepts for a more complex manned mission to Mars. He published the *Mars Project* in 1952, with concepts as detailed as those for the lunar mission. Although his plans involved gigantic undertakings, von Braun calculated everything with precision. Before his technical plans for a human mission to Mars became a reality, von Braun had already written a science fiction novel covering the topic, but his manuscript was rejected by publishers. He did not give up on it, however. He was aware that a greater public interest could help him negotiate better opportunities in his attempt to make his projects a reality. Later, he started to publish small chapters of the novel in magazines, in an attempt to popularize his *Mars Project* by illustrating key aspects and bringing them to the attention of the public. The book was eventually published in print in 2006 with the title *Project MARS: A Technical Tale*.

Open to any opportunities that could help him advance his work, von Braun started to work with Walt Disney as a technical director for Disney Studios, producing three films about space exploration. As the first television film to talk about the topic, *Man in Space* gathered an audience of 40 million viewers upon its debut on March 9, 1955. The series continued with two other successful films that also gathered a large audience. In 1959, von Braun's efforts concentrated on publishing a short booklet on an updated concept for a manned lunar mission with only one small spacecraft piloted by two astronauts.

Von Braun was disappointed to realize that the American government was not interested in his dreams of space travel and had very modest goals when it came to rocketry. Moreover, accounts of the press about his past in Nazi Germany were taking the focus away from his scientific pursuits. Early in 1956, the priority shifted at Redstone Arsenal to the development of the Jupiter intermediate-range ballistic missile (IRBM) with a range of 1200 miles. Von Braun and his team were placed under the Army Ballistic Missile Agency (ABMA), headed by the soon-to-be Major General John Medaris.

The world changed on October 4, 1957, when the Soviet Union successfully launched the *Sputnik* satellite into low Earth orbit. The small benign satellite, about the size of a beach ball, orbited the Earth and emitted a pulse of radio "beeps" that were literally heard around the world. The satellite kept broadcasting the radio signal for 21 days until the battery on board ran out. A cry came out from the public: Why was America so far behind the Soviets in space? A month after the first *Sputnik*, the Soviets launched *Sputnik II*, which carried a much larger 1,120 pound payload that included a dog named Laika.

The United States, worried about lagging behind the Soviet Union, assigned von Braun and his team the task of building an orbital launch vehicle. Their experience in working with missiles made them the perfect candidates to undertake such a daunting endeavor. After the impressive success of the Redstone rocket, the team started to work on the Jupiter-C. Although von Braun worked on several projects during this period, the most important was the development of Jupiter-C, a modified Redstone rocket, which on January 31, 1958, launched the first satellite of the Western world, *Explorer 1*. The Explorer satellite weighed 30.8 pounds and orbited the Earth every 114 minutes. Radio signals from the satellite's transmitters were picked up shortly after launch. The satellite had the scientific mission of measuring cosmic radiation and sending the data back to Earth. After the successful launch of Explorer, an exuberant von Braun told reporters at an early morning press conference, "We have firmly established our foothold in space. We will never give it up again." The event marked the beginning of a new era for the United States and it is considered the birth of the space program.

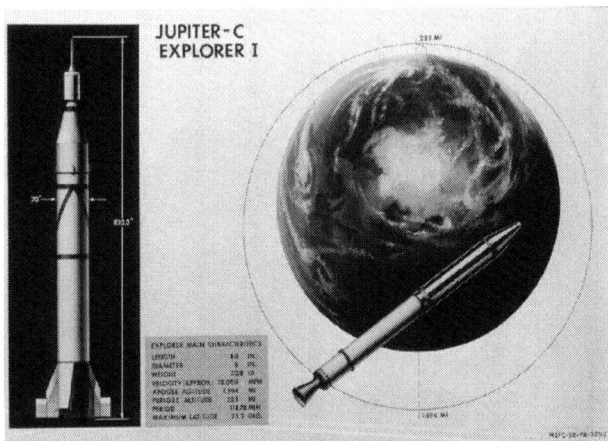

Figure – This illustration shows the main characteristics of the Jupiter C launch vehicle and its payload, the Explorer I satellite.

The Soviet Union clearly had the early lead on the exploration of space and the United Sates was determined to gain superiority over the Soviets in this new frontier. The Senate Majority Leader Lyndon Johnson was a supporter of giving space exploration a high priority. President Eisenhower, with half-hearted support, sent Congress a proposal to establish a national space agency. Congress passed the Space Act in mid-July to create the National Aeronautics and Space Administration

(NASA) to be headquartered at Langley, Virginia. President Eisenhower signed the measure into law later that month and appointed Keith Glennan as the new agency's first administrator. Von Braun went to Washington, D.C., late that summer for a private meeting with the new director.

In late 1959, NASA's administrator Glennan made a formal request to transfer the ABMA group to the new space agency. By the middle of 1960, all but a small number of von Braun's division had transferred under the NASA umbrella. Von Braun became director of the newly created George C. Marshall Space Flight Center (MSFC) in Huntsville. The main business of the center was to develop propulsion systems for space vehicles. The newly created MSFC was given a sprawling eighteen-hundred-acre portion of the Redstone Arsenal and became NASA's largest center in staff and budget. Von Braun would remain director of the MSFC until 1970.

The newly formed Marshall Space Flight Center went to work on the rockets that would propel the Mercury-Redstone manned space capsule. Before man could travel into space, a series of unmanned test launches were planned, which were to be followed by animal passengers. 1961 saw the chimps "Ham" and "Enos" launched into space, which was all in preparation for the planned launch of what would be the first human into space, Alan Shepard. Once again, the Soviets beat the Americans to the punch when Air Force Major Yuri

Gagarin safely orbited the Earth in a five-ton space craft. Soviet Premier Nikita Khrushchev spoke to the orbiting Gagarin boasting, "Let the capitalist countries catch up with our country."

Von Braun and his team at Marshall went into high gear to regain some of the ground lost to the Soviets. Just three weeks after Gagarin's historic flight, Navy Commander Alan Shepard climbed into the single man Mercury capsule atop a Redstone rocket at Cape Canaveral, Florida. The capsule that Shepard was to ride in was a product of NASA's Manned Spacecraft Center near Houston, Texas. On May 5, the mini-spaceship with Shepard was launched into an arcing fifteen-minute ride traveling 116 miles up and back in a matter of minutes. Though this was not the accomplishment of an Earth orbiting mission that the Soviets had completed with Gagarin, it did put, although briefly, the first American into space.

Chapter 6 - Race to the Moon

"One good test is worth a thousand expert opinions." - Wernher von Braun

Just weeks after Alan Shepard's historic flight, President Kennedy threw America into an all-out race to the Moon when on May 25, 1961, he spoke to a joint session of Congress on the country's future in space. President Kennedy challenged the nation in his speech:

"...First, I believe that this nation should commit itself to achieving the goal, before this decade is out, of landing a man on the Moon and returning him safely to the Earth. No single space project in this period will be more impressive to mankind, or more important for the long-range exploration of space; and none will be so difficult or expensive to accomplish. We propose to accelerate the development of the appropriate lunar spacecraft. We propose to develop alternate liquid and solid fuel boosters, much larger than any now being developed, until certain which is superior. We propose additional funds for other engine development and for unmanned explorations— explorations which are particularly important for one purpose which this nation will never overlook: the survival of the man who first makes this daring flight. But in a very real sense, it will not be one man going to the Moon—if we make this judgment

affirmatively, it will be an entire nation. For all of us must work to put him there…"

Von Braun and his key people gathered in the main conference room at Marshall to hear the speech. Von Braun publicly praised Kennedy's challenge to the nation. However, not everyone was as enamored with Kennedy's speech as von Braun. Former president Eisenhower called Project Apollo "a mad effort to win a stunt race. To spend $40 billion to be the first to reach the Moon is just nuts!"

Figure – President Kennedy delivers a speech challenging the nation to go to the Moon. May 25, 1961.

To place a man on the Moon would require the accelerated development of the heavy lift Saturn family of rockets. The development of the Saturn rockets, the Marshall Center's first major mission, took von Braun a step closer to his dream of manned Moon flights. After a series of disappointing tests and experiments, the Marshall Center's first important success was the development of Saturn rockets able to transfer heavy loads beyond Earth's orbit. The maiden test flight of a Saturn I rocket came in October of 1961. This was the first in a series of three version of the heavy-duty space launch vehicles developed by von Braun's Marshall Center team for Apollo, Skylab, and the joint Apollo-Soyuz manned orbital mission with the Soviets. The Saturn rocket was a leap forward in rocket development with a cluster of eight engines of its first stage generating an enormous seven million pounds of thrust. Once the Saturn rockets were developed successfully, the team of scientists and engineers moved forward to the Apollo program. In 1962, von Braun developed the lunar orbit rendezvous concept, working closely with former Peenemünde teammate, Kurt H. Debus, who was the first director of the Kennedy Space Center.

In the summer of 1966, von Braun traveled to Antarctica, together with other members of NASA's top management, to meet the U.S. scientific and technological community who had the mission of exploring the Antarctic wastelands. Von Braun believed that the insights provided by the researchers in Antarctica could be useful for his missions of manned space exploration. He was interested in understanding the management of the research stations and wanted detailed accounts about logistics, habitation, and life support. He also wanted to test essential equipment on the barren Antarctic terrain such as glacial dry valleys, making sure that the equipment was adequate for extreme conditions, similar to those expected on other planets.

Von Braun's childhood dream of helping humankind set foot on the Moon was accomplished on July 16, 1969, when the Saturn V rocket launched the Apollo 11 crew on a historic eight-day mission that took astronauts to the Moon. The Saturn V rocket was an engineering marvel, standing almost 365 feet tall including the Apollo spacecraft. The giant rocket weighing in at over six million pounds had more than three million parts, with each stage containing more than seventy miles of electrical wiring. NASA Administrator Glennan described the super rocket as "one of the most amazing combinations of engineering, plumbing, and plain hope anyone could image."

Apollo 11 was the spaceflight that landed the first two humans on the Moon. Mission commander Neil Armstrong and pilot Buzz Aldrin landed the lunar module Eagle on July 20, 1969. Armstrong became the first to step onto the lunar surface six hours after landing; Aldrin joined him about 20 minutes later. They spent nearly three hours together outside the spacecraft and collected 47.5 pounds of lunar material to bring back to Earth. Michael Collins piloted the command module *Columbia* alone in lunar orbit while they were on the Moon's surface.

Armstrong and Aldrin spent just under a day on the lunar surface before rejoining *Columbia* in lunar orbit. On July 23, the last night before splashdown, the three astronauts made a television broadcast in which Collins commented, "The Saturn V rocket, which put us in orbit, is an incredibly complicated piece of machinery, every piece of which worked flawlessly... We have always had confidence that this equipment will work properly. All this is possible only through the blood, sweat, and tears of a number of a people... All you see is the three of us, but beneath the surface are thousands and thousands of others, and to all of those, I would like to say, 'Thank you very much.' "

Six other teams of astronauts reached the surface on the Moon with the help of Saturn V rockets during the entire course of the Apollo program. Von Braun confessed after the success of the Apollo flights that before and during those crucial moments he would pray a lot. After the first Moon landing, he talked optimistically to the public about the possibility to launch manned missions to Mars in the next decade. After the Apollo program ended, the American enthusiasm for space travel waned — the Moon had been conquered and there was no grand goal on the horizon to rouse the public and the policymakers who held the purse strings to fund such adventures into space.

Figure – Saturn V launching Apollo 11 capsule to the Moon on July 16, 1969

Von Braun's merits in the development of the U.S. Space and Rocket Center in Huntsville were recognized by the entire scientific community. His contribution was essential also for the launching of the Applications Technology Satellite, a program that von Braun wanted to expand in India with the purpose of launching an education television project for the poorest communities of the country.

On March 1, 1970, von Braun and his family moved to Washington, D.C., where he was appointed NASA's Deputy Associate Administrator for Planning. Only two years later, after a series of internal conflicts and severe budget cuts, von Braun retired from NASA, disappointed that his visions for the future of space flight were incompatible with NASA's agenda. Once the goal of reaching the Moon had been accomplished, the interest for manned space exploration dropped dramatically. Shortly after, von Braun became Vice President for Engineering and Development at Fairchild Industries, an aerospace company from Germantown, Maryland. In 1976, he joined the Daimler-Benz board of directors and became the personal consultant in scientific matters of Lutz Kayser, CEO of OTRAG. As his health began to deteriorate, von Braun was forced to retire completely in 1976.

Besides his work as a scientist and engineer, von Braun was also an advocate for space technologies and science. He was the mind behind the development of Space Camp, the program that engaged generations of children by providing them training in the fields of space exploration technologies. Von Braun was a firm believer that children needed mental development as much as they needed physical development. He also founded and developed the National Space Institute.

Von Braun has received worldwide recognition for his work in the Apollo program. Sam Philips, the director of the Apollo mission, declared that without von Braun, the United States would most probably have never reached the moon. To honor von

Braun's memory, a large crater on the Moon was named after him.

Chapter 7 - Personal Life

"I have learned to use the word 'impossible' with the greatest caution." - Wernher von Braun

Wernher von Braun, for all his brilliance and great accomplishments, had his share of shortcomings — some amusing and others not so much. During his many travels, he enjoyed staying up late drinking whiskey and smoking with the "boys." Von Braun's assistant, Tom Shaner, recalled, "He was definitely a night person and notorious for not getting up early." On more than one occasion Shaner had to go up to von Braun's hotel room door and pound on it until he would eventually answer, "Yes, yes. I will be right down." Shaner said, "I would make him walk to the door and open it. He would be standing there in his shorts right out of bed. He hadn't taken a shower, he hadn't shaved... So I learned not to trust Dr. von Braun when would say he was up."

Over the years von Braun's media star rose to the point where he would be recognized virtually anywhere he traveled in the world. Von Braun's persona flew in the face of many of his serious-minded colleagues who received little recognition for their hard work and dedication. The friction between von Braun and his colleagues was summed up by an aerospace scientist named Herbert Friedman, who spoke of von Braun: "an affable person with a friendly personality [who] certainly had the capability to charm people." However, "Many of us resented him because he would appear [at meetings]...and monopolize the stage. He was always followed by media people, and he could disrupt a meeting very thoroughly just by being there... I was put off by his public image."

In the midst of World War II in 1943, he decided to marry Dorothee Brill, a teacher in Berlin, but his mother opposed the marriage. At the end of 1943, he got into an affair with a French woman, but their relationship became impossible when she was imprisoned for collaboration at the end of the war. Once in America living at Fort Bliss, von Braun sent a marriage proposal letter to Maria Luise von Quistorp, his maternal first cousin. In 1947, von Braun flew back to his country and married her in a Lutheran church in Germany. Werhner von Braun was 35, and his much younger bride was 18. After the wedding, the new couple expected a restful German honeymoon alone, but much to their surprise, when they returned to their room there were two U.S. military police waiting for them. The MPs were there to prevent the scientist from being kidnapped by the Soviets. The newlyweds had no choice but to accept their new round-the-clock houseguests. He returned to the United States with his wife and his parents. He and Maria Luise had two daughters and a son.

Once the von Braun's set up their household in Huntsville, they became active in the community. Maria was outgoing; in addition to raising three children, she earned her pilot's license, attended horse shows in Tennessee and elsewhere, enjoyed water sports, and pursued her love of travel, attended concerts, and toured museums as opportunities arose.

Von Braun became increasingly religious during his time in the United States and he underwent a conversion from Lutheranism to evangelical Christianity. While living in Germany, von Braun had been a non-practicing Lutheran who never took religion seriously. During his younger years, he never showed interest in religious matters. In 1946, invited by a neighbor, he attended a church in El Paso, Texas, where he was living at the time. Although he accepted the invitation out of mere curiosity, he discovered a lively community that impressed him, making him realize that religion included discipline and effort, two things he valued greatly. In his later years, von Braun became an advocate of his religious beliefs, especially in writing and public speeches. He became an active member of an Episcopal congregation and often spoke publicly about the need to reconcile science and religion.

Figure – The von Braun family circa 1955

Although in 1973 von Braun was diagnosed with kidney cancer during a routine medical examination, he continued his work unrestrained, traveling all over the country to speak at colleges and universities. Above all, he wanted to cultivate an interest in spaceflight and rocketry among children and students, hoping to encourage them to become the next successful generation of aerospace engineers. In January 1977, the gravely ill von Braun resigned from Fairchild Industries. Later that year, outgoing President Ford awarded von Braun the nation's highest honor a scientist can receive, the National Medal of Science in Engineering. His deteriorating health prevented him from attending the White House ceremony in his honor. Instead, von Braun's longtime friend Edward Uhl presented the medal to him in a private ceremony in von Braun's hospital room. Von Braun, with tears in his eyes, said, "Isn't this a great country? I came here with all that I owned in a cardboard box, somewhere between a former enemy and not yet a citizen, and we were given all the opportunities of citizenship. The country has treated me so well and now the president is giving me this high honor."

Von Braun spent the final weeks of his life in the hospital with "his last credo" being, "Thy will be done," his favorite passage for the Lord's Prayer. Wernher von Braun finally succumbed to cancer and died on June 16, 1977, at his home in Alexandria, Virginia. He was buried in Ivy Hill Cemetery, in a churchyard in Alexandria, Virginia. Present at the graveside were his family and a few friends. The simple headstone was engraved: WERNHER VON BRAUN, 1912-1977, Psalms 19:1. The citation on the headstone was an old testament verse which was a longtime favorite of his: "The heavens declare the glory of God; and the firmament showeth His handiwork."

The End

Thank you for reading this book. I hope you enjoyed it. Please leave a review of the book; I read each one and they help me become a better writer. Doug

Timeline

March 23, 1912 - Birth of Wernher Magnus Maximiliam Freiherr von Braun.

1930 - Serves as a volunteer apprentice to a group of rocket experimenters in Berlin headed by Hermann Oberth.

1932 - Graduates with a Bachelor's degree in aeronautical engineering, after which he joins the University of Berlin to study Physics.

1934 - Receives his Ph.D. in Physics from the University of Berlin.

October 3, 1942 - First successful launch of an A-4(V-2) rocket.

August 17, 1943 - Royal Air Force bombing raid on Peenemünde kills 735 people, wounding hundreds more.

March 1944 - Is detained by Gestapo for two weeks.

May 2, 1945 - Von Braun and his team surrender to the U.S. Army.

December 8, 1948 - The von Braun's first child is born, Iris Careen.

May 8, 1952 - The von Braun's second daughter, Margrit Cécile, is born.

October 18, 1952 - Von Braun's article, "The Journey," appears in *Collier's* magazine as part of a special issue titled *Man on the Moon.*

1952 - Becomes the technical head of the U.S. Army Ordnance Guided Missile Project in Alabama, where his team successfully launches Jupiter-C, Redstone, Pershing, and Juno missiles.

1954 - Von Braun works with Walt Disney to produce educational videos about space exploration.

April 14, 1955 - Wernher and Maria von Braun become naturalized citizens of the United States.

October 4, 1957 - The Soviet Union launches the first artificial Earth satellite *Sputnik I* into low Earth orbit.

January 1958 - Von Braun and his team launch the first American artificial Earth satellite, Explorer I.

June 2, 1960 - The von Braun's son Peter Constantine is born.

September 8, 1960 - President Dwight Eisenhower visits formal opening ceremony of NASA George C. Marshall Space Flight Center in Huntsville, Alabama.

May 25, 1961 - President Kennedy gives speech to a joint session of Congress challenging the nation to put a man on the Moon and return him safely to Earth by the end of the decade.

July 20, 1969 - Neil Armstrong and Buzz Aldrin become the first humans to walk on the Moon as part of the Apollo II mission.

1960 to 1970 - Director of the Marshall Space Flight Center.

1970 to 1972 – NASA Deputy Associate Administrator for Planning in Washington, D.C.

July 1, 1972 - Becomes the vice president of Fairchild Industries aerospace company.

1975 - Receives the prestigious National Medal of Science, which is awarded in 1977.

December 31, 1976 - Resigns from Fairchild Industries due to health problems.

June 16, 1977 - Dies of cancer.

Acknowledgments

I would like to thank Lisa Zahn and Andreea Mihaela for help in preparation of this book. All photographs are from the public domain. The quotes at the beginning of each chapter are from Brainyquote.com.

References and Further Reading

Neufeld, M.J. *Von Braun – Dreamer of Space, Engineer of War*. Vintage Books, New York. 2007.

Taylor, J.W.R. and K. Munson. *History of Aviation*. Crown Publishers, Inc. New York. 1977.
Ward, B. *Dr. Space: The Life of Wernher von Braun*. Annapolis, MD: Naval Institute Press. 2005.

West, D. *Dr. Robert H. Goddard – A Brief Biography - Father of American Rocketry and the Space Age*. C&D Publications. 2017.

"Excerpt from the 'Special Message to the Congress on Urgent National Needs' " Accessed August 5, 2017.
https://www.nasa.gov/vision/space/features/jfk_spe ech_text.html

About the Author

Doug West is a retired aerospace engineer, small business owner, and experienced non-fiction writer with several books to his credit. His writing interests are general, with expertise in science, history, biographies, numismatics, and "How-to" topics. Doug has a B.S. in Physics from the Missouri School of Science and Technology and a Ph.D. in General Engineering from Oklahoma State University. He lives with his wife and little dog, "Scrappy," near Kansas City, Missouri. Additional books by Doug West can be found at http://www.amazon.com/Doug-West/e/B00961PJ8M.
Follow the author on Facebook at
https://www.facebook.com/30minutebooks.

Figure – Doug West (photo by Karina Cinnante-West)

Additional Books by Doug West

Buying and Selling Silver Bullion Like a Pro
How to Write, Publish, and Market Your Own Audio Book
A Short Biography of the Scientist Sir Isaac Newton
A Short Biography of the Astronomer Edwin Hubble
Galileo Galilei – A Short Biography
Benjamin Franklin – A Short Biography
The Astronomer Cecilia Payne-Gaposchkin – A Short Biography
The American Revolutionary War – A Short History
Coinage of the United States – A Short History
John Adams – A Short Biography
In the Footsteps of Columbus (Annotated) Introduction and Biography Included (with Annie J. Cannon)
Alexander Hamilton – Illustrated and Annotated (with Charles A. Conant)
Harlow Shapley – Biography of an Astronomer
Alexander Hamilton – A Short Biography
The Great Depression – A Short History
Jesse Owens, Adolf Hitler and the 1936 Summer Olympics
Thomas Jefferson – A Short Biography
Gold of My Father – A Short Tale of Adventure
Making Your Money Grow with Dividend Paying Stocks – Revised Edition
The French and Indian War – A Short History
The Mathematician John Forbes Nash Jr. – A Short Biography

The British Prime Minister Margaret Thatcher – A Short Biography
Vice President Mike Pence – A Short Biography
President Jimmy Carter – A Short Biography
President Ronald Reagan – A Short Biography
President George H. W. Bush – A Short Biography
Dr. Robert H. Goddard – A Brief Biography - Father of American Rocketry and the Space Age
Richard Nixon: A Short Biography - 37th President of the United States
Charles Lindbergh: A Short Biography - Famed Aviator and Environmentalist

Index

38693818R00035

Printed in Great Britain
by Amazon